From Street Block to Cell Block

The Choice Is Yours

Michael A. Mason

© Copyright 2019, Michael A. Mason

All rights reserved. No part of this book may be used or reproduced by any means, graphic, electronic, or mechanical, including photocopying, recording, taping or by any information storage retrieval system without the written permission of the publisher except in the case of brief quotations embodied in critical articles and reviews.

ISBN: 978-0-578-50561-9 (soft cover)

Published by:
Fideli Publishing, Inc.
119 W Morgan St.
Martinsville, IN 46151
888-343-3542

www.FideliPublishing.com

For bulk orders, please contact
Kearia Patterson via phone 219-276-7416
or via email: keariashontell1@yahoo.com.

DEDICATIONS

This book is dedicated to the young men who need help finding their way. I want you to know it's never too late to change. It's all up to you.

In addition, I dedicate this to my sons, Michael Mason Jr. and Patrick Mason. You loved me when I didn't love myself.

To my Mom, your son has finally realized his potential, and I'm using it in a positive way. I pray I've made you proud.

ACKNOWLEDGEMENTS

To Roderick Gunn,
My Pastor, Editor, and Friend

To John Allen, you came through when I needed you.

RESOLUTION

I, Michael Mason, do solemnly pledge before God to give my all to the youths of today and tomorrow. I will be honest in my teachings, guidance, and in everything I do. I promise to walk in integrity to honor God.

I make this commitment to help you in becoming a man of integrity with great value to yourself, your family, and the community. I will love you, serve you, and teach you how to become a man of honor. My goal is to show you Your Life Matters and to teach you how to love yourself. I will work diligently in providing the guidance you need to succeed in life. I will never abandon you because you're a precious gift from God. I will give my all to accomplish the mission God has given me; to save and preserve your life for His kingdom. I, therefore, appeal unto you: Young Man Listen!

Vowed this 31st day of July, 2018

Signature: *Michael Mason*

CONTENTS

Introduction ix

Who Do You Love? 1

The Streets 13

Prison 27

Your Life Matters 41

Study Guide 53

    Day 1: Who Do You Love? 55

    Day 2: Who Do You Love? 57

    Day 3: The Streets 61

    Day 4: Prison 65

    Day 5: Your Life Matters 67

Open Letter to My Family 69

INTRODUCTION

I wrote this book for the young men who are searching for guidance, as someone who cares. This is not an ordinary book and it's not written in an ordinary way. I didn't write this for your parents or your teacher. It was written specifically for you, young man. Your mother will never be able to understand where I'm coming from. Your father, most likely, isn't there or too embarrassed to talk about the things I'll share with you.

If you give me a chance, I'll give you an explicit look into the world you know nothing about but desire to be part of. I'll make no attempt to glorify it or sugarcoat it. I want you to see the ugliness, loneliness, fear, and shame that comes with the street life.

Brothers, I'll give you a first-hand account about the choices we make. Coming from someone who has lived the life you desire. A lot of people will express things to you they haven't experienced. Though they mean well, you don't need someone who has never driven a car telling you how to drive.

I'm speaking as someone who has experienced what you are going through, or may be planning to engage in. I pray, by reading this, you would be deterred from the path of experiencing the things I've went through resulting in 21 years behind bars. I'll show you how one wrong decision can impact your life forever.

I avoided writing this book for years due to the responsibility that comes with the role of a mentor and an inspired role model. The stakes are so high. I feared failing, where my failures could contribute to lives lost. My prior failures caused mothers to mourn for their children, who were never afforded a chance to live out their fullest potential. God showed me by not writing this book, I had already failed mothers, fathers, and their children. He revealed that those children were never given a chance because I withheld such opportunities.

What's written in this book will save lives, families, and, most importantly, your life. I want to save the culture, minimize, eliminate and stop the cycle of you killing each other. I will give you a clear perspective about the choices you make and their future consequences. I know you are tired of people telling you, you'll either end up dead or in jail. However, has anyone ever told you, when you die, you don't die alone? A part of a mother and father goes to the grave when they bury a child. Has anyone ever told you, if you go to prison, your family will be doing time also? I will show you the detrimental effects your actions will have on their lives and the lives of your siblings.

I've never read where the truth was told about the street life and prison. No one wants to talk about the pain and suffering because they are too embarrassed. No one explains how you could lose everything and everyone when you go to prison. I will show you the reality of true friendship from false friendship; how people will stop accepting your calls when you go away, and how your child could end up calling another man Daddy. This is not an urban novel nor is it a rap song which so many of you base your lives on. If you want to label it, call it a reality check. This is the undeniable truth about where you are heading as young men if you don't straighten up.

I've spent 21 years in prison because no one took the time to explain these things to me. That's why I'm taking the time to explain them to you, to give you the chance I didn't have. It's up to you what you'll do with it. If you want to save yourself and your family from the unbearable pain and suffering that comes with the street life, this book is for you. If you want to survive your teenage years, follow me. I will assist you in becoming a man of integrity, with morals, and principles you can pass on to your children. Those of you reading this, yet refuse to take heed, you are the ones who will most likely die in the streets or spend the majority of your lives in prison. On the other hand, some of you will read this book, apply the lessons, and give yourselves a chance at succeeding.

I'll pull back the curtain to help you confront your fears. I'll expose the street life and prison culture so you can make educated decisions about your life. You need to know that you can discuss your fears. Everyone has them. Most young people do things out of fear and peer pressure; things they really don't want to do. The sad thing is they never tell anyone. How many times have you heard your friends say they were scared? Probably never. The funny thing is, if they told you they were afraid in a certain situation, you'd probably say "me too." I told a friend how scared I was of writing this book. He told me, "If you wasn't scared, then you shouldn't write it." He explained my fear came from my passion for what I desired to write about and not making a difference in anyone's life. I'm asking you give God a chance to help me help save your life so you can succeed and fulfill your destiny.

WHO
DO YOU
LOVE?

Who do you love?

Before you start this next chapter, ask yourself these questions and write down your answers.

1. Who do you love?
   _____

2. How do you show them?
   _____

3. Is it really love you're showing them?
   _____

4. Do you mislead those you love?
   _____

5. Are your parents proud of you?
   _____

6. Are you someone your siblings should look up to?
   _____

7. Do you love anyone enough to change?
   _____

8. Do you love yourself enough to change?
   _____

9. What will it take for you to change?
   _____

10. Do you want to live beyond your teenage years?
    _____

WHO DO YOU LOVE?

When most young men are asked this question, they usually give the same answer. They will quickly tell you how much they love their mothers, fathers, sisters, brothers, and grandparents. The next question I ask is, "How do you show them?" That's where the problem comes in. For the most part, you don't know how to love or express yourselves and somewhere along the line you've been taught some crazy concepts about love. You believe jeopardizing your lives expresses your love, when that is so far from the truth. You've been taught that love is about sacrificing, which is true, as long as you're making the right sacrifices.

Most of you have a misconception of the meaning of love or what it means to love someone. You were raised to believe that love is how someone makes you feel. However, love is an action. It is the act of sacrificing for the comfort and well-being of those you say you love. Some mothers work two jobs to make ends meet, sacrificing their time and health because they love you. Parents deny themselves the pleasures of life so you can have them. That's love. Love gives; it is patient and kind. It's not

> **Love gives;
> it is patient and kind.
> It's not selfish and it never fails.**

selfish and it never fails. So, do you truly love yourself, and your family? *Who do you love?*

What I'm about to share with you, most people don't like to hear. Every young man I've shared this with in prison stopped talking to me for a couple of weeks because the truth hurts. You might put this book down after you read this. All I ask is, once you have settled down and accepted the reality of what I've said, pick the book up again and continue this journey.

You say you love your mother. Right? Well why do you hurt her so much? Why do you cause her so much heartache and pain? Why does she have to live in fear for your life? I remember when I was first arrested and called my mother. She said something I'll never forget: "Well, at least I can sleep at night now and don't have to worry about someone calling me in the middle of the night telling me you were found dead somewhere." Wow! This was coming from the woman I loved most in life. I did not know what I was doing to her; I did not know my actions burdened her so much.

I had no idea my actions were slowly killing my mother. Do you ever think about that? I know I didn't. It hurts me so bad when I think about what I've done to her. After I lost at trial, the judge sentenced me to three life sentences plus 30 years consecutive. When my mother came to see me, she said, "I wish I could switch places with you and do your time." She would do anything for me, even after all of the things I'd put her through.

My attempt here is to get you to open your eyes, heart, and mind. I don't want you to use ignorance as an excuse any longer. You know what your actions are doing to your loved ones. So, STOP IT!

At some point in life, you'll be held accountable. I pray you can live with the decisions you make, because they affect so many people you say you love. Let me ask you a few questions. *Do you care about your mother enough to change? Are you man enough to show your mother how much you love her?* Ask yourself these questions, because only you can answer them. Only you can decide what you're going to do. I sincerely pray you'll make the right decision.

Everyone loves grandma, so they say. Yet you disrespect your grandmother so much that she becomes ashamed of you. Some grandmothers are so ashamed of their grandsons' conduct, they refuse to go around their friends. They fear what might be said about their grandson's lifestyle. Your grandmother may be fearful of what someone will tell her you've done, while she struggles, or has struggled to raise you.

> *You know what your actions are doing to your loved ones.*
> *So, STOP IT!*

Both she, and your mother, sacrificed so much for you, but you talk to them in such disrespectful ways. The funny thing is, you probably have more respect for your father, who may have been missing out of your life or in prison, than you do for those who have been there for you. Think about that. *Who do you love?*

Have you ever been in a car, glanced back, and the police were behind you? Do you remember the fear that overcame you, especially if you were dirty? Were you ever committing some crime and heard those sirens getting closer? You know that feeling you get. Take a minute to think about what went through your mind then.

Now let me take you somewhere else. Think about how your mother's heart rate increases whenever she hears gunshots, because you are in the streets. She has no idea where you are or what you're doing. Think about how fearful she becomes when she sees a police car with someone in the back seat. Would you believe she becomes fearful to look, hoping it's not you in the back seat? Do you know that you cause your mother sleepless nights and high blood pressure? Do you realize your actions can cause her to age faster? *Who do you love?*

If your mother is alive, is she proud of you? Can she brag to her friends about you or does she stay away from friends to avoid talking about you? I talk about mothers and grandmothers because they are the only ones most of you had growing up. They are the ones you wanted to make proud. At some point in your lives you lost sight of that; it became more about you and less about them. You need to get back that love and devotion. Show them that they can still trust and believe in you.

Do you remember when a loved one lost your trust? When you realized you couldn't trust them, how did you feel? How does your mother feel knowing she can't trust you? If you're in this position, it's not too late to change that. You can earn back her trust. You can still make her proud. You can allow her to cry tears of joy instead of tears of sorrow.

So, what will you do? How will you move forward? Will you become someone that she can be proud of? *Who do you love?*

All of you love your sisters and brothers, especially the younger ones who look up to you. You love them, yet, continue to ruin their lives by misleading them. If you are a younger brother, you know exactly what I'm talking about. Think about how much you looked up to your older brother or how much your younger brother looks up to you. He wants to be just like you because he thinks you're so cool. Your younger sister will grow up wanting to be with someone like you because she thinks you're cool.

Do you see how your path directs their path? Most times, when we try something new, it's because someone we look up to has done it and they're someone we want to impress. That someone is you when it comes to your siblings. Those with older brothers can testify to this. Are you in a position now because you tried to be like or impress your older brother? Is that the reason for your poor decisions? Will you continue to put your younger brother or sister in the same position?

It doesn't necessarily have to be your siblings, it can be anyone who looks up to you as a role model. Give them a real chance at life by setting good examples. Let go of the selfish mentality of thinking about yourself and start thinking about your loved ones. I know you love your siblings.

We all do. You just don't take the time to think about your actions. Think about how they'll affect them. That's all I'm asking you to do. *Who do you love?*

My oldest brother got his girlfriend pregnant at 17 years old. When he turned 18, he went into the Navy to be able to take care of his son. He was the only positive male influence I had in my life. When he left for the Navy, I started selling drugs. When he came home for a two-week leave, I hid from him. He was so mad and disappointed in me.

For the past 21 years, he worked for the same company and earns $105,000 a year. During those same 21 years, I sat in a prison cell. The skills he obtained from the Navy set him on this path; a path he tried to lead me onto. My brother, Johnny Frazier, is the perfect example of a big brother. Even with his faults, he was a good brother, a good husband to his wife until the day she died, and a good father to his children and mine, too. Can anyone say the same thing about you? Or will you end up like me, praying your children find someone of a positive influence to raise them?

I've given some of my best years to the prison system and what I have left, I'm giving to you. I want to save you, the same way my brother wanted to save me. Please don't run from what I'm saying like I ran from my brother. If you ask me, "Who do you love?" I would say, "YOU!" That's why I wrote this book. *Who do you love?*

Now let's talk about fathers for a minute because they are so important to who you are and who you'll become. A father is responsible for raising his son and teaching him how to be a man. He's there to instill in you the morals and principles that will help you navigate through life. Without this guidance, you will be lost.

Many young men are lost because their fathers failed them. You were left to raise yourselves or your mother and grandmother stepped in to do a job only a man can do. I'm not taking anything from those females who may have raised you but, at the end of the day, I can't teach a young lady how to become a woman and they can't teach you how to become a man. That doesn't stop them from giving you their best, which creates a bond that should never be broken or forgotten.

Somewhere along the line that bond was lost and you don't even realize it. You may be thinking I'm crazy right now because you'll always love and respect them. Yet, your actions say something different. Your actions say you really don't care about them. On a daily basis, your actions say, "I don't care if I hurt you." Your actions say, "I want you to feel my pain of growing up fatherless." Here's the funny thing, some of you wanted to become better men than your fathers; while most of you end up just like them or even worse.

How does a father tell his child that he doesn't love them? How can he tell his child, "I don't want to be there for you"? I know you're telling yourself you would never say those things to your child, but when you choose the streets, that's exactly what you're saying. You're telling your child the streets are more important than him or her. Don't get upset or think that I'm judging you. Remember, I've missed 21 years of my sons' lives. The only difference between you and me is, nobody told me.

> ## *Quit lying to yourself and acting like everything is okay.*

How did it feel when this happened to you, when your father chose the streets or something else over you? Can you see where your anger comes from; the lack of respect you have for others? At what point did you stop valuing life? Some of you have given up and are throwing your life away. You live as if there's no tomorrow and you don't care about today. *Who do you love?*

If you have children, take a minute to think about them. Think about how much they need you now, and in the years to come. You know how important it is for you to be there, in the same manner it was important for your father to be there. I know you grew up with the desire to become a good father, son, grandson, and friend. You may have promised yourself you would make your mother proud. "WHAT HAPPENED?" I pray you would ask yourself that question, and be honest with yourself.

Quit lying to yourself and acting like everything is okay. The last two generations have been fatherless and we have to stop that. I want you to be there to raise your children. I want you to live long enough to have them, but you have to give yourself a chance. *Who do you love?*

Brothers, quit jeopardizing your lives for nothing. Stop living as if your life is over when you haven't even begun to live. Love someone besides yourself and allow them to love you. Give yourself to your family, not the streets. Give those who look up to you the same chance I'm giving you today; a chance at surviving.

Please don't wait until you end up in prison to start listening. Invest in saving yourself and your family. Start thinking before you act. Most importantly, start loving yourself. *Who do you love?*

After reading this chapter and reflecting on it, return to the questions at the beginning of the chapter. Answer each question again and see if your answers are the same. If they are, I suggest you read this chapter again.

THE STREETS

The Streets

Before you start this chapter, ask yourself these questions and write down your answers.

1. What do you really know about the streets?
   _____

2. Are you willing to sacrifice your family for the streets?
   _____

3. Are you willing to give up your life?
   _____

4. Do you realize within three years of entering the streets, it's a chance you'll either end up dead or in jail?
   _____

5. Will you listen to the warnings that life sends your way?
   _____

6. Do you want to make it through this storm in your life right now?
   _____

7. Are you prepared to save yourself and you family?
   _____

8. Are you man enough to change?
   _____

9 Do you want to live every day in fear for your life?
   _____

10. Do you care if you live or die?
    _____

THE STREETS

Some of you are considering a life in the streets. If so, I suggest you talk to someone who has experienced the street life and has changed their way of living. Speak to someone older than you; someone you believe will be honest. The lust of the street life is unexplainable and unfounded anywhere else. At the same time, it demands your all, even what you refuse to give.

There's not much you can do in life that will cost you everything. When I say everything, I mean *every-thing*. A lot of you have already lost family, friends, and dreams to the streets. You've lost what little morals and principles you had and before you know it, you'll lose your soul. The streets demand everything out of you and it won't be satisfied until it gets EVERYTHING.

> *The streets demand everything out of you and it won't be satisfied until it gets EVERYTHING!*

It doesn't matter who you are. You'll live your life not trusting anyone; not family nor friends. There is nothing I can tell you to express the feeling of the fear you live with in the streets. Most people murdered in the streets are murdered by someone they know. Their so-called friends are people they chose to let into their lives and hang around with. Those same people, whom you've fought beside and protected, will be the first to tell on you when confronted with criminal charges and prison time.

You really have no idea what you're getting into. Luckily for you, this is the information age. So, research what you're getting into. Most people won't tell you the truth about it, so check the facts. I'm not asking you to believe me; do the research yourself. Your life depends on it; the well-being of your loved ones depends on it. Consequently, when you enter the street life, you take them with you. Their safety, health, and well-being will be greatly affected the moment you step into that zone. The street life is a killer that shows no mercy to its members or those they love.

The most important thing in a man's life is the people he surrounds himself with. So, choose your friends wisely. If your friends are selling drugs, then guess what. You'll eventually start selling drugs. If your friends are in gangs, then you're on your way to becoming a gang member, too. So, is it time to find some new friends?

There's a warning before every storm to let you know what's heading your way. **This is yours.**

In some storms, people lose everything and never recover. Those who do recover, do so by the grace of God. The only reason I'm able to share these things with you is because of God's grace. Without it, I would still be in prison covering my face while my celly uses the toilet.

I spent all those years in prison because of the decisions I made and the people I chose to run with. I'll never blame anyone for what happened to me. I made my own decisions. So, before you make any kind of decision, be sure you can live with the consequences of those decisions. Be sure that your family can live with them also. In most cases they're unable to or refuse to. At times, family members become so disappointed that they abandon those in prison. Yet, the hard-to- accept reality is that you abandoned them first when you chose the streets. You showed no regard for them or their feelings. So, they'll show no regard for yours. You want them to do the right thing but, you wouldn't. You want them to show how much they love you, yet you refused to show them.

The streets are filled with so much ugliness hiding behind the glitz and glamour. You need to know, it's not a game. Mothers rent out their daughters for a hit of drugs. You may look up one day and find your best friend's mother or sister offering you their body for a hit of drugs. I've seen a man rob his grandmother just to get high. There's nothing in the streets that hasn't been done and won't be done. Fathers rape their daughters, while high on drugs and didn't know what they were doing. Your best friend will set you up to be killed out of jealousy because he wants your girl. I've watched a man walk up on his own mother as she was being passed around by his so-called friends. You will even find sons selling drugs to their own mothers.

I've seen this so many times, yet I still don't understand it. They would say, "If she doesn't get it from me, she'll get it from someone else." Could you become that person? Could you sell drugs to your mother? This is the reality of the streets. Once the curtains are pulled back, you'll be sickened by what you find. These are things no one wants you to see. They know if you find out before you commit yourself, you'll run away as fast as you can.

You can never see the loneliness a man feels while he's running in the streets but, it's there and it's unbearable, especially if he's getting some real money. You can't trust anyone out there — not your brother, woman, or best friend. Everyone is suspect when it comes to that paper. The same reason some people love you will make others hate you. Nobody wins in the streets but the streets. Your best friend will have your wife and kids kidnapped while you're hustling or kicking it together. Your wife or girlfriend will pretend to be kidnapped by a guy she's sleeping with just to get him some of your money. You can't trust anyone because everyone wants or needs something.

Could you imagine living your life and not being able to trust anyone; not being able to talk to anyone or count on anyone? Those you could count on, you gave up for the streets. There's no love in the streets, only loneliness and distrust. The only person you can trust in the streets is yourself. So, you're forced to separate yourself from everyone else.

> *Nobody wins in the streets but the streets.*

You're alone out there, just like you're alone in prison. The only person who will be with you that you can trust is God. Some people become so paranoid, they refuse to trust Him. You never know what's behind a man's smile. It could be love, hate, envy, distrust, or solitude. Most of the time you don't even want to know because it may cost you your life.

In the streets, you live in fear in order to survive. You have to watch everyone because everyone is a suspect. You're on the lookout for the police, stick up boys, haters, and those closest to you. Your fear keeps you on point but it also makes you paranoid and unstable. Those who don't live in fear are easy preys. Likewise, you also live in constant fear for your family because if they can't get you, they'll settle for them. No one is safe or off limits in the streets.

Once the street gets hold of you, you'll become a different person. You'll do things you wouldn't normally do. At some point, you'll become ashamed of yourself. A lot of things you'll do will be kept to yourself, until you learn to stop caring. During my incarceration, I rarely talked about my street life, because I was embarrassed. I wasn't proud of myself then and I'm not proud of the "old me." I'm ashamed to share some of the things I've done in the streets with my sons. I'll have to live with this shame for the rest of my life. No matter how old I become or how much I've changed, I can never forget who I was and the things I've done. No one else may know the things you've done, but they'll always bear heavily on your conscience. It's something you'll have to live with.

How many people have you seen murdered in the streets? I'm talking about your friends or someone you know. How many times have you said to yourself, "That could have been me?" Are you going to continue

> *No matter how old I become or how much I've changed, I can never forget who I was and the things I've done.*

living this lifestyle until it is you? Until you are the one lying in the middle of the street bleeding to death or looking out from the back seat of a police car?

Before every storm there's a warning to give you an idea of what is coming. Are you going to prepare yourself or will you continue to maintain the status quo of the streets? In the event you've decided to stay the course, please be advised: You'll take your family into the storm with you. If you are murdered or sent to prison, your family will be affected. You leave them no option but to deal with the mess you created out of selfishness.

For Jesus loves us, he gave his life so we could have life. What will you do for those you say you love? Start preparing yourself to avoid this storm. I know you can hear the alarms and sirens going off. SAVE YOURSELF!

Ask your mother or someone you respect about those individuals they know who chose the street life. Ask them where those individuals are today. I bet they're either dead, strung out on drugs, or in and out of prison. Very few people make it out of the streets. Most people in the streets have, roughly, a three-year run before they are murdered or sent to prison. Meaning within three years of entering the street life, you'll either be in jail or dead.

So, when you think about it, for one to three years of so-called fun, you'll sacrifice your life to the prison system, drugs, or the grave and in some cases all three. What kind of trade is that? It doesn't add up. The end results (drug addiction, prison, death) don't justify the means. This isn't life, no matter what angle you look at it. This type of lifestyle can be easily categorized as: Suicide (killing of one's self), Genocide (extermination of people), Homicide (killing of a human being by another), Infanticide (killing of an infant), and Demoralization (killing morale), and Destiny Derailment (killing destiny). My attempt here is to open your eyes and give you some understanding from my experiences and the pain produced by my past choices.

If after reading this book you still decide to embrace the streets, then I want you to know you've chosen death and destruction for yourself and your family. I pray that you are not murdered out there. Although, there may come a day you'll be sitting in a jail cell thinking about this message you chose to ignore. Just consider yourself lucky you are still alive. I do hope you'll be strong enough to make it through your sentence, because a lot of men aren't.

There are two things the streets and prison promise you: darkness and destruction. Now, here's one final thought: No man or woman, who loves themselves, would ever give their life to the streets. Trust me. I know.

> *No man or woman, who loves themselves, would ever give their life to the streets.*

After reading this chapter and reflecting on it, return to the questions at the beginning of the chapter. Answer each question again and see if your answers are the same. If they are, I suggest you read the chapter again.

PRISON

Prison

Before you start this chapter, ask yourself these question and write down your answers.

1. Do you value your privacy?
   _____

2. Are you willing to live in a restroom?
   _____

3. Do you have any respect for yourself?
   _____

4. Do you have any morals and principles?
   _____

5. Would you like to keep them?
   _____

6. Do you like to be told what to do and when to do it?
   _____

7. Do you mind being strip searched?
   _____

8. Would you like to spend your life feeling abandoned?
   _____

9. Do you have any real friendships?
   _____

10. Do you want to spend majority of your life in prison?
    _____

PRISON

What I'll share now is my 21-year experience behind bars. If doing time was a job, I'd be retired. This experience is filled with suffering, fear, and embarrassment. There's so much that comes with doing time and none of it is good.

I was sentenced to die in prison. I was given three life sentences without the possibility of parole. So, my fear and reality for almost 20 years was I would die in prison.

I've spent nearly half of my life alone and afraid. I went to bed every night with this weight on my shoulders and no one to help carry the load. I lost my mother in 2004, my father in 2005, and the woman I loved in 2006. I mourned for them alone because there's no love in prison and

> *There's so much that comes with doing time and none of it is good.*

no one to comfort you. Whatever you go through in prison, you face by yourself. You'll hide your pain until you can't bare it any longer and end up hurting someone or forcing someone to hurt you.

A lot of you will go to prison at a young age and you won't be able to control your sexual desires. Your desires will become so uncontrollable that they'll start to play with your mind. You'll eventually begin to have delusions, and start thinking the female staff likes you. You'll began to tell yourself that she wants to see your manhood.

This has caused many to expose themselves to female staff, anywhere, around anyone, which led to masturbation. They become so sick and delusional that they have no regard for that female or anyone else around. The sad part is, it doesn't bother them that the female is someone's mother, sister, wife, or daughter. All they think about is their sexual desires. Desires that often lead them to seek comfort from other men, engaging in disgusting activities.

Some of you may say, "I'll never do those things." You'll never imagine becoming the man you'll turn out to be in prison. The good thing is, you don't have to. You never have to see that place. You never have to put yourself in a position to compromise your values and morals. The decisions you make in prison are life changing and detrimental.

Everyone considers themselves men, and men do what they want, when they want. Well, *not in prison!* The only thing you have control of in prison is your mouth and your response. You better control them both or the consequences could be dire.

Prison is nothing to brag about. In fact, I'm embarrassed because so many people mislead you about that, and I was one of them. I remember one day I was watching the hit television show *Empire*. Terrence Howard's character made a statement I'll never forget. He said, "When you go to jail, that makes you a [G], but when you go to the Feds that makes you an [OG]." This was the dumbest thing I'd ever heard. I thought about the millions of young men who watched this show and were misled. I was embarrassed, because I knew this was the type of stuff you're being fed. No one corrected or contradicted this statement or spoke the truth about prison.

The hardest thing to do in prison is to be a man. Someone is always trying you one way or another. You're always making compromises and it's extremely difficult to be yourself.

I'm sure you've heard people talking about prison and what they've done behind bars, but has anyone ever told you how they cried when they were alone in their cell? Has anyone told you how they begged God to help them with their situation? No one wants to be viewed as weak in prison. You are taught only the strong survive, and in a lot of ways that's true. I'm exposing my experiences, hoping you'll get some real insight into the life you are setting yourself up for. The saddest thing to see in prison is a grown man afraid and he thinks no one knows.

The only time you can admit you're afraid is when you are alone with God. However, He already knows how afraid you are of wasting away in prison. He knows you're not the person you pretend to be. He knows you need his help but you're afraid of what your so-called friends may think. He knows how lost you are. He's just waiting for you to turn over your life to him.

> *In prison, the only time you can admit you're afraid is when you are alone with God.*

You wouldn't believe the quantity of drugs that circulate within the prison walls. Brothers become addicts out of boredom, or fear of facing their reality. They got high because there was nothing else to do, and before you know it, they're addicted.

Some days behind bars you'll feel like you're in the show *The Walking Dead,* because everyone walks around looking like zombies, high on drugs and they can't tell you what that drug is. They smoked a piece of paper or a piece of cardboard that drove them crazy. A lot of times their bodies rejected whatever they took and you never know what's going to happen. I've seen a young man fall to the ground claiming he could no longer feel his legs. Another returned to his childhood, crying for his bottle. I've witnessed a brother wash his face in the toilet, then drink some of the water. I've seen young men strip naked and walk into the dayroom as if they're fully clothed. Those who were still around the next morning didn't remember what they had done while they were high.

I watched these men and became so disgusted, until I realized I was looking at myself in my younger days. The only difference, I got high with weed or intoxicated by alcohol. It made me wonder how people looked at me with disgust, instead of trying to help me. I decided right then I would help, instead of sitting back and judging you or them. It's so easy to judge someone, but it takes courage and passion to help them. As I shared earlier, I was afraid of writing this book, but I stepped out in courage and faith. I wrote this book because I love you, because I fear for you and because I used to be you.

One day a young man came to my cell and told me he had 20 days left before he was going to be released. He told me he had seven little girls, and two were in foster care. He explained how he wanted to get custody of his girls in foster care. As he sat there talking, I noticed he was high. At some point he asked if I had any advice for him. I told him: "Yes. Do not go home and bother those little girls because you're coming right back to prison." I explained that if he got custody of those little girls, every time he went to prison, his little girls will go with him — meaning back into foster care. I can still see the expression on his face. He left my cell very upset because I told him the truth. If he was in prison getting high, then he would go home and continue to get high. I told him he didn't love those two little girls or the other five either. I told him how selfish he was. If he could, he probably would have beat me up. That wouldn't have changed my mind or how I felt.

> *It's so easy to judge someone, but it takes courage and passion to help them.*

There is no way for me to express the loneliness you'll feel in prison. Even though you are always around someone, you will always feel alone. True friends are hard to find in prison, so you're surrounded by so-called homies; other men who are just as lost as you are. In most situations in prison the blind lead the blind. Ninety percent of prisoners answer to someone else, known as a shot caller. He's the person who makes the decisions for the inmates from that state, gang, or what is called a car. If the shot caller tells you to stab someone, you have to stab that person or be stabbed yourself. If he tells you to hold the knives, then you have to hold them.

Right now, you may be thinking no one can tell you what to do. I've seen so many young men enter the system thinking like that, but they never lasted long. I've seen young men, who upon entering the cell house, you could smell fear coming from them. What made it even worse is there's nowhere to hide. You are surrounded by men with no regard for life; they care about no one, especially not you.

The fortunate young men who enter the prison system are those who have family support, at least until they chase them off. Maybe some of your friends will stick around and support you. Most people will abandon you, slowly forgetting about you and moving on with their lives. Prisoner's girls sometimes end up with so-called friends of theirs, who most definitely changes their minds about the relationship. This means they'll stop accepting your phone calls.

Your child may end up calling another man daddy. You'll be too ashamed to tell anyone and just keep it to yourself. You'll end up calling home, asking someone to send you some money. They'll tell you yes, but never send it. Sometimes, the only one who wants to be bothered with you is God.

Slowly, you'll start to realize and accept what's going on in your life. Before you know it, you'll find yourself just being alive, but not living. After a time, nothing will have any meaning to you, because everyone has shown you that you have no meaning to them. You'll hide your feelings and what you're going through because you don't want anyone to know how everything is affecting you. God knows. He'll be there when everyone else abandons you. He saved me and he can save you if you give Him a chance.

In prison, you basically live in a restroom with beds inside, which would be okay, if someone else didn't share the cell with you. Some prisons have timers on the showers and toilets, where you get a limited amount of water, and a few flushes every 30 minutes. You must remember that you live in the cell with someone else and during lock down, you're in the room when he releases his bowels. He only gets one flush every three minutes while you're only a few feet away, under your blanket, covered from head to toe to minimize the incoming stench. If he flushes twice in three minutes, he won't be able to flush again for 30 minutes. He may have to pour Kool-Aid or shampoo into the toilet to kill the smell until he can flush again. This is the life you'll get by choosing the streets.

> *Sometimes, the only one who wants to be bothered with you is God.*

I know you've heard of "Stop and Frisk," which the court held as unconstitutional in the State of New York. Did you know they also have "Stop and Frisk" in prison? However, they take it a step further than just patting you down. An officer can strip search you whenever he feels the need to. If you've never had the pleasure of a strip search, allow me to walk you through one.

There's always at least two officers present as you remove every piece of clothing you have on, while passing each piece to them to be searched. Once that's done, you have to open your mouth wide so they can search inside to make sure you're not hiding anything there. Next, they'll check inside and behind your ears, then your hands, and under your arms.

Throughout the strip search, you're standing there stark naked. You'll feel so embarrassed and violated, but that's not the worst part. Eventually, you have to lift your genitals and move them around so they can verify that you're not hiding anything there. Next, you'll turn around and raise each foot and wiggle your toes.

Yet, the most humiliating part is when you're told to squat, spread your cheeks, and hold them open while you cough three times as they look at your butt-hole to make sure there's nothing there. Then, you're handed your clothes and told to get dressed.

No matter how fast you get dressed or how many pieces of clothing you put on, you'll still feel naked. Every time you see the officers who put you through this, you'll feel humiliated and violated. Just think about this for a moment; they can do this to you the next day if they want to.

Every time you go on a visit to see your family and upon returning, you have to submit yourself to a strip search. In order to spend some

> *Don't wait until you're in a prison cell before you decide to change.*

quality time with your family, you must be violated. This is for those fortunate enough to get visits.

You have no privacy in prison, except in your mind, and some people have lost that. I can't understand why no one has ever shared these things with you. Maybe, it's because they are too embarrassed to tell you how other men have made them squat and cough while they stared up their butt. Believe me, I'm embarrassed also, but I want to save *you* the embarrassment even more. I'm embarrassed the way young men are throwing away their lives. I'm embarrassed you don't value your life or anyone else's.

At some point, you'll have to start making better decisions to avoid these situations. Your decisions will determine who you are. Your decisions will determine if you'll experience the things I just shared with you. Only you can make those decisions, but you're not the only one who has to live with them; they will affect your family also. Don't wait until you're in a prison cell before you decide to change. Decide right now, to become a better son, brother, father, and friend to those you love. Decide today that you won't give your life to the prison system. Make a conscious decision today to initiate change in your life.

After reading this chapter and reflecting on it, return to the questions at the beginning of the chapter. Answer each question again and see if your answers are the same. If they are, I suggest you read this chapter again.

YOUR
LIFE
MATTERS

Your Life Matters

Before you start this chapter, ask yourself these questions, and write down your answers.

1. Do you believe that Your Life Matters?
   _____

2. Do you live like it matters?
   _____

3. Do you value the lives of other young men like yourself?
   _____

4. Do you live, expecting to die, at a young age?
   _____

5. Do you have a bad attitude?
   _____

6. Are you affected by that disease called Pride?
   _____

7. Can you control your temper?
   _____

8. Do you think about how the decision you make will affect your family?
   _____

9. Do you desire to become a good role model?
   _____

10. Will you start believing in yourself?
    _____

YOUR LIFE MATTERS

When someone is murdered in the streets by a police officer, there's an uproar. You protest and riot throughout the communities. The mothers of these men are broadcasted on the news demanding justice, with attorneys flying in from all over the country to represent them. All of this, because YOUR LIFE MATTERS. My question is, "Why does it seem like the only time your lives matter is when they are taken by the police?" What about the hundreds of lives taken daily by young men like yourself? Those lives should matter, too. So, what's the reason for this outrage, when you murder each other daily? Why the protest and news conferences? Why do you act like it's okay to kill each other?

Look at it like this: If you ask a mother whose child was murdered by the police, and you ask a mother whose child was murdered by one of their peers, I bet they'll tell you their pain was the same. They both loved their child and think he didn't deserve to die. Both mothers valued their child's life, regardless of who murdered them. Every mother who has

> *Until you start respecting yourself, no one else will.*

lost a child in the streets should be treated and supported just as Michael Brown's mother was supported, because every child's life matters.

YOUR LIFE MATTERS, whether you believe it or not. If you don't believe it, no one else will. If you don't start living like YOUR LIFE MATTERS, you'll continue to kill each other.

Why don't you value your life? What happened to make you think so low of yourself? Until you start valuing your life, you'll never be able to value the lives of others. I know your environment and circumstances have discouraged you and have you thinking less of yourself than you should. As a result, you've allowed everyone else to think less of you. No one will ever know who you are until you find out who you are. Until you start respecting yourself, no one else will.

How can you expect anyone else to take you seriously, when you don't take yourself seriously? You fight and kill each other for anything and about anything. Because you don't value life, most of you are just existing, taking up space, waiting for someone to take your life. That's sad, but it's true. It's accepted as the norm for you to die young.

It doesn't have to end that way. Your life doesn't have to be that way. I pray that you will allow the words herein to change the direction you're heading. I want to change your perspective on life so you can dream again. With your help, we can make the communities safe again. We can make the atmosphere of our communities safe havens where kids aren't afraid to go to school or the corner store; a place where they don't fear they may be shot. They shouldn't have to live like that, in torment and fear. THEIR LIVES MATTER! So does yours, if you would just believe it.

In prison, there's a program with the attached mission statement, "Attitude is everything." Those words are so true, especially when you recognize it and make it a daily application to your life. Your attitude will put you in certain situations and it's your attitude that will get you out of them. If you have a bad attitude in the streets or in prison, then most likely you'll have a vast amount of problems. Your attitude determines how people interact with you and treat you. In some situations, your attitude will determine whether you live or die. So, yes attitude is everything. If you don't check it, someone else will.

Do you have a bad attitude? Is that the reason you live, as if, your life doesn't matter? If so, that has to change.

To change your attitude, you have to change your way of thinking and your perspective. Most people's attitudes are derived from past and present situations. Attitudes are also developed from beliefs. Beliefs stimulate emotions and irrational thoughts. Some people allow their past to determine who they are.

When I decided I wanted to change, the first thing I had to adjust was my attitude. Most of the trouble I've had in life was caused by my attitude. When I changed my attitude, things got better in my relationship with God, my family, and my fellow man. Yes, attitude is everything.

> *A good attitude can help you accomplish everything.*

A good attitude can help you accomplish everything. A bad attitude can destroy your accomplishments. So, check your attitude before you address the other areas in your life.

Here is a list of attitudes you should be eager to develop: Gratitude, Responsibility, Open Mindedness, Caring, Honesty, Humility, Loving Kindness, Willingness, Patience, and Commitment. Although none of this will mean anything, until you believe YOUR LIFE MATTERS.

Young men suffer from one of the greatest diseases in the world and don't even know it. It has killed more people than cancer and AIDS. This disease is called Pride. I know you're thinking Pride is not a disease, but I'm here to tell you different. This disease will spread throughout your entire being and destroy everything it touches — your character, perspective, attitude, and your responses. However, if you recognize it early and get the proper treatment, you may survive. It causes much pain for you and your family. Sometimes medicine won't help because you are too far gone. Sounds like Cancer, doesn't it? However, it's Pride I'm talking about. Pride does to your character what Cancer does to the body without your knowledge of it. Pride just kills you faster.

How many people have been murdered because they refused to walk away, because they didn't want to look bad? That was Pride.

How many fights have you seen because someone didn't back down? That was Pride.

Pride is the number one cause of death among young men.

If it wasn't robbery when someone was murdered in the streets, then most likely pride was involved. When someone is murdered in prison, pride is involved. If you think about it and put things into perspective, you'll see it plain as day. Pride forces you to do things you don't want to do and say things you really don't mean.

How many times has your pride or ego gotten you into trouble? Pride destroys families, relationships, and friendships. Are you carrying the Pride virus around? Are you allowing your Pride to destroy something you love? Will you continue to allow this disease to eat away inside of you? To stop this disease from spreading, it'll take a lot of work and prayer. You can fight and beat this thing called Pride. You have to kill this virus before it kills you, as it did so many others. To do so, you must learn the art of humility and change your thought process because YOUR LIFE MATTERS.

When your car runs hot, everyone knows you don't open the cap on the radiator immediately or the hot fluid will shoot out everywhere, burning you and others. That radiator is your emotions and the cap is

> *Pride is the number one cause of death among young men.*

your mouth. If you don't let the radiator [you and your emotions] cool down before you open the cap [your mouth], things will explode and people will get hurt.

How many times have you opened your mouth before you cooled down? How many times have you said things and wished you hadn't? One thing about words, once they're released, you can never take them back. No matter how many times you say, "I'm sorry," it won't change the effects of your words.

You can tell when you are about to run hot [explode, lose control]. For instance, when I'm getting upset, my body temperature changes and I become sweaty. I learned to control myself when this happens, by removing myself from the situation before I open my cap [my mouth]. Do you know when to pull over and cool off? If not, then pay attention the next time you are in a situation and recognize your turning point, because we all have one. Our mind, soul, and body are designed to give pre-warnings that our radiator is about to overheat.

My time in prison was harder on my sons than it was on me because I've been a failure as a father and provider. I never had the pleasure of dropping them off at school or picking them up. I've never been to a school play or a basketball game. I wasn't available to teach them how to ride a bike or defend themselves. The birthdays I was able to share with them, they were too young to remember. For 21 years, I was nothing but a voice on the phone to them. A voice of a man they heard utter thousands of times how much he loved them but never showed them.

Will you do the same thing to your children? I'm trying to stop you from becoming that voice on the phone. I'm trying to show you how to get the love you deserve, by showing your love ones the love they deserve.

Those of you who have played the role of the child in this situation know it's not easy. You don't have to evolve into playing the role of the father also. If this cycle has already begun in your family, you have to stop it. Use the same energy and determination you were going to invest into the streets into saving your family. You can either stop it yourself or God will.

I spent over 21 years of my life in prison because God stopped a cycle in my life before it could get started. My younger brother and I were the first ones in our family to go to prison and we were the last. God changed the course of our destiny before we destroyed our family with our street life. Don't force Him to do the same thing to you. I learned the hard way but you don't have to. You don't have to give your life to save theirs. You can live your life to save theirs by setting a good example. Show them that THEIR LIVES MATTER and so does yours.

My children don't know each other. They've been around each other but don't know each other. There's a huge gap between them caused by my absence. It's called "sibling separation." This is just another fruit of my incarceration and its effects on my family. Please think about the decisions you make, not only for yourself but for your family also, because YOUR LIFE MATTERS. Don't wait until you're in the back of a police car or lying in the streets bleeding to think about your parents or children. You're given an opportunity while reading this book.

I remember going to McDonalds, back in the day, when I saw a guy working the drive-thru who was just in class with me earlier that day. I laughed at him while I sat in my new car. I thought I was better than him because I didn't have to work at McDonalds to get money. I also thought I was smarter than him.

Those individuals I used to laugh at, became real fathers to their children. They had the opportunity to take them to school, attend their games, and teach them how to become respectable young men and women. They never missed a birthday, Christmas, PTA meeting, or graduation. They were the ones who showed their children how much they loved them. They were the ones who showed their children that THEIR LIVES MATTER. So, who was smarter and better? It definitely wasn't me, that's for sure.

In life, you pay for your experiences and most of the time pain is the price. Do you have any idea how much pain you've caused yourself and blamed others for? Until you start taking responsibility for your actions and believing YOUR LIFE MATTERS, you'll never understand this.

It causes me great pain when I see you throwing away your life, because I was once you and I know what you are about to go through. I know what you're about to put your family through, especially if you have children.

I don't know you personally but I've seen you a thousand times before. I've shared a cell with some of you. Some of you have come into my cell and requested prayer. I've seen some of you so afraid that I became afraid for you and wanted to protect you. I've seen on the news how you murder each other in the streets. I've dreamt about you so many nights, waking up in cold sweats. I pray for you every night, asking God to help you change your lives. No, I don't know you personally but I've known

> *I want you to succeed, make your mothers proud, and become proud of yourselves. Most importantly, I want you to realize YOUR LIFE MATTERS.*

you all of my life; you just have different names and faces. When I cry for you, I don't see a face, name, or color. What I see is my lost young brother who needs to understand that HIS LIFE MATTERS.

Brothers, I dream of you being a positive impact in the lives of others, just as I desire to be one in yours. I visualize you as leaders in this country. I imagine you loving yourselves and others. My desire is to watch over you as you become better men, sons, brothers, and fathers. My greatest desire is that you would embrace this truth and allow it to be lived out from a humble attitude. Invest in yourself; believe YOUR LIFE MATTERS and live in victory.

I told you at the beginning this wasn't an ordinary book. I told you this book wasn't for your parents or teachers. I wrote this book for you, God's children because your sins have been forgiven on the account of Jesus' name. Embrace this truth and make it your reality. I'm writing to you fathers, because your children need you. Your community needs you. It's time to pay your dues. I'm writing to you young men because I love you and I want you to overcome the temptations of the street life and fast money. I want to see you succeed and make your mothers proud. I want you to become proud of yourselves. Most importantly, I want you to realize YOUR LIFE MATTERS.

STUDY GUIDE

STUDY GUIDE

Thank you for taking the time to read this book. You've taken the first step in changing your life. Now, I ask you to bear with me a little while longer to give you this opportunity to make things right in your life. In this study, you will address your parents, siblings, and most importantly yourself. Put it all on the line for those that love you. Open your heart, mind, and soul, to bring about this new birth.

I pray this study helps you in a very profound way. I pray your love ones will be able to see the difference in you. I pray there will be a difference in you.

Note for instructors: If this book is used in a study group, I encourage the instructor to follow-up with the participants every 60 days. If there's an area a young man needs help or encouragement in, then revisit that chapter. By showing this level of interest, you will continue to encourage the group to change and show that you care. Too many times we provide the information and expect them to do the rest on their own. Let's not only set out to change them, let's change ourselves.

WHO DO YOU LOVE

DAY 1

After reading this chapter, I'm sure you're left with some questions and a heavy heart. I know this because we all love someone, even if we don't know how to show them. If you're wondering where you go from here, and you want to start showing your love ones how much you love them, then commit yourself to this.

It's so hard for young men to express their true feelings, because to express your feelings requires honesty. Young men find it so hard to look someone in the eyes and say, "I love you and I'm sorry." That's okay. We'll get through this together.

If you've answered the questions at the beginning and end of these chapters, then you're ready to move forward. By answering those questions, you've acknowledged there are some things you need to share with those you love; things you should no longer keep to yourself for the sake of those you love.

Knowing how hard it is for you to express yourselves openly, here's a compromise. Instead of telling someone how you feel and how sorry you are, I challenge you to write this person a letter. It could be a letter expressing your love and apologies to your mother, grandmother, or some other authority figure in your life. It could be a caregiver whom you've disappointed by your actions or someone you want to tell how much you love and appreciate them but don't know how. I encourage you to write this letter for the following reasons:

1. The person you write this letter to can always go back and read it to remind themselves how much you love them as often as they want to and whenever they want to.

2. You can upload it or send a copy of it to your phone as a reminder. Something to refer to when you're struggling with some decisions in your life.

3. Those of you who apply these life lessons and succeed will always be able to look back and see where you came from, and how much you have grown.

Please take the time today to express your feeling to someone you love.

WHO DO YOU LOVE

DAY 2

Yesterday, you wrote a letter to at least one of your caregivers expressing your love and apologies. How did that make you feel? Were you honest? I'm sure you've touched their hearts with your letters. I know what it must have done for you. I wrote some people in my life after 18 years in prison, apologizing for things I'd done 20 years prior. I felt so relieved and free afterwards. I commend you on the steps you've taken so far.

For some of you, there's someone who desires to hear from you even more than your caregiver. Possibly, your siblings or those who look up to you and want to follow in your footsteps. They need to hear from you because, whether you know it or not, their lives are in your hands. So, what are you going to do about it? I want you to write them a letter also.

Some of you are in a position where that's all you can do at this time. For those of you in that position, I suggest you start writing today. Don't quit after your first letter. One letter won't do it. Become consistent with your inspiration and guidance. While you're changing your life, allow them to see those changes in your letters.

For those who are able to sit down and communicate with your siblings or those who look up to you on a daily basis, you've got your hands full. You are in a position to change lives. Not only your life, but the lives of those around you, the lives of those you love. When you allow them to see the change in you, they'll know what you're saying is real. They'll see that you love them and want the best for them. As a result, you'll be able to change the things you exposed them to.

Most of you are in a position where you can give them something you didn't have, someone to speak positively into their lives. As you prepare yourself to become a better example, I want you to ask yourself these questions.

1. What do I need to change about myself to help change others?

   _____

2. Am I willing to give enough of myself to change others?

   _____

3. Am I serious about saving myself and those I love?

   _____

4. Will I stop misleading those that look up to me?

   _____

5. Am I committed to stop them from making the same mistakes I've made?

   _____

Once you've come to terms with yourself and understand your mission in life, you'll be able to help others with theirs. If your answers to the previous questions are no, then you should continue to work on yourself before you attempt to help someone else. Please be aware that every day counts when you're influencing someone else's life. Just when you may think you're ready, you may find out it's too late.

THE STREETS

DAY 3

When I talk about the streets, I'm talking about the criminal lifestyle in general. No matter where you come from, the consequences and repercussions are the same. The fear and pain are found everywhere. So please don't just read this section with the mentality that it's not for you. This section could possibly save your life.

Young man it's time for you to do some soul searching. It's time to decide who you are and who you want to become. You can start by answering these questions.

1. Do you want to live life not being able to trust anyone?

   _____

2. Do you want people to be able to trust you?

   _____

3. When you make a decision, do you think about anyone else and how that decision will affect them?
   _____

4. Do you want to live life alone in constant fear?
   _____

5. Can you tell what's behind a man's smile? Most importantly, what's behind yours?
   _____

6. Are you man enough to save your family, by saving yourself?
   _____

7. How many of your friends have been murdered in the streets?
   _____

8. How many of your friends are sitting in jail or a juvenile facility as you read this?
   _____

9. What will you do and sacrifice for those you love?
   _____

10. Will you choose a life of death and destruction or a life of prosperity and love?
    _____

I pray you answer the above questions truthfully. Please don't lie to yourself. If you don't like your answers then you can change them by changing yourself and the decisions you'll make thereafter. You've been granted a chance some generations before you didn't get. God is giving you another chance to survive and to escape a death trap.

This is a blueprint, an inside look into darkness. You've been given a chance to stop and evaluate yourself and the street life before you throw your life away. I wish I was given this opportunity when I was your age. You don't have to end up like so many of us did. No one told us, so please HEED THIS WARNING because the storm is coming.

PRISON

DAY 4

I pray that as you read this you're not in jail or prison. However, if you are, then what you just read is a reality for you. For those who are not incarcerated, I pray you'll never have to experience being locked up. I pray you'll never have to experience the things I've shared in this chapter. Prison is a painful experience for everyone, whether they want to admit or not. As I stated before, it's also an experience some of you will never have to endure and for others, an experience they should never have to endure again.

You've written a letter and answered some questions; now it's time for you to read and reflect. Today I would like you to read the chapter on Prison again; don't just read it, reflect on it. Close your eyes and visualize certain situations mentioned, then decide if that's what you want for yourself. Please don't cheat yourself by just breezing through this, because the decisions you make today will bring their own consequences tomorrow. If you take this seriously, it can impact your mind, heart, and soul in positive ways.

If you apply yourself to this exercise and honestly reflect on the message, it could save your life. It can also save your family. You should engage in this, as if your life depends on it, because in some ways it does.

Brothers as you reflect on this chapter, I encourage you to remember this is not a movie, rap song, or urban novel — this is your life and when you hear those bars close, you'll know it's real.

YOUR LIFE MATTERS

DAY 5

Your life matters — if I could get you to believe this, everything else would be so much easier. It would be easier for you and your family. Everything you've read so far, every question you've answered, and every thought and reflection boils down to this: Do you believe YOUR LIFE MATTERS?

As you read this chapter, I'm sure you could hear my heart being poured out to you through the pages. If you were touched by those words, then I know you felt my passion. There's nothing more important to me than saving you. I don't care what other people are going to say about what I wrote. I want you to know the truth, YOUR LIFE MATTERS.

Attitude is everything! I know after reading this section, you came to realize how true that statement is. I just pray you are prepared and willing to make the proper adjustments in your attitude to succeed in life. Pride is a virus we've all carried at some point in our life. I'm a Pride survivor and you can be one also. All you have to do is give God a chance to work on your character and attitude. Only then, will you have meaning and purpose in life.

What I'm about to ask you to do will seem so simple, yet challenging. It's as serious as anything you've ever done. You can lie to me, your mother, grandmother, or anyone else, but you can't lie to yourself without being conscience-stricken.

I want you to write a letter to yourself. A letter explaining how you feel right now, about your actions in the past, and the steps you'll take to move forward. Please don't rush through this, because it will become your blueprint. Upon completion, make an extra copy and give it to someone you love. You don't have to let anyone else read it, if you don't want to, this is strictly for you. However, if you have no confidence in holding yourself accountable, then give a copy to that someone I mentioned above to hold you accountable. This will be your accountability partner.

As I mentioned prior, your "Letter-to-Self" can be strictly for your eyes only. I encourage you to upload it onto your phone as a reminder of the commitment you've made to yourself and your family. You've read mine, now I challenge you to write yours. I can't tell you what you're going to do from this point on, only you can do that. So, you will have to hold yourself accountable for what you write. You must remember your siblings and parents are watching and counting on you. They want to trust and believe in you again. Show them that YOUR LIFE MATTERS.

AN OPEN LETTER TO MY FAMILY

For the past two months, I've been upset and mad at God. This morning, I started thinking about Momma having to raise eight kids on her own. How could she not be mad? But she never showed it. She never blamed us for the situation she was in nor did she complain. She lived for her children, and died not knowing how special she was to us. Today she can look down on us and feel what we didn't know how to show her then.

When God called her home, he called her to rest. God was such a great friend to her that he said, "Barbara, come and go with Me. I want to show you something." He took her to heaven with Him so she could look down and see what she couldn't see from here — a family who truly loved and cherished her, a family who still, to this day, is trying to get it right, in spite of the things we've gotten wrong. Yes, a family of her making.

I remember she asked me where I got my courage from, not realizing that it came from her.

To show you how good God truly is, he told Michelle, "I think you're lonely and tired. Come up here and spend some time with Me and your mother." So, he took her home and allowed her to see what she couldn't see from here. He allowed her to see that her children loved her dearly. They just didn't know how to show it.

During her transition home, God gave Rob an opportunity to open his heart; to love and care for our sister like no other man ever has.

Linda, you started out in an abusive relationship, a relationship that eventually pushed you into the arms of the Lord. You've been holding on tight to Him ever since. You honored and respected God to the point that I began to fear you and I didn't even know God. It wasn't hard to see what He'd done for you. You ended up raising three God-fearing young ladies and a strong young man.

Glynda, you were born with a short leg and you wore braces until you got it together. For most of your life you've walked without them, although you walked with a limp. As you got older it wasn't easy, especially with all of the burdens you've carried over the years.

One day you heard a whisper, a little small voice telling you, "Come let Me carry your burdens. Let Me be your strength when you are weak." He's been carrying you ever since. He's changed you in ways you couldn't even imagine. Continue to thank and praise Him for what He's done in your life.

Brenda, you were born with dyslexia, causing you to spell everything backwards. You never let that stop you because He never let it stop you. Not only did you overcome it, you've spent your life helping others in the same situation. God blessed you so that you could be a blessing to others, and that you are!

I spoke of these things because there is something I want you guys to understand along with everyone else who reads this. I want you to know that you're "CONQUERORS" because you took what the devil threw at you, picked it up, and threw it right back at him. You've raised a generation of conquerors. Guess what else? You got it from Momma!!!

Johnny, you were born in an environment in which you weren't expected to survive. That was the excuse so many of us used, but not you. You became a man before your time and that's what makes you the man you are today. Thank you for being the man I could never be. Although we chose different paths, I pray that we'll end up at the same destination. I love you, Johnny. Thanks for being there for my son.

Rob, I love you dearly whether you know it or not. I looked up to you when I was young, but you've also disappointed me over the years. For the past couple of years, you've been the brother I can look up to again. The way you stepped up for Michelle and Grandma is amazing. I'm actually jealous because I don't know if I could do any better. I never knew you could be so caring. I'm so proud of you. You've earned your big brother status back and you make me proud to be a Mason again.

Eric, you followed me for most of your life, even into prison. I just thank and praise God that He didn't allow me to lead you to an early grave.

Grandma, you've been my mother, grandmother, and friend for so long. You've never heard me curse and that's something I pride myself on. I take pride in that because I always wanted you to know no matter how old I got, you'll always be my grandmother and you'll always be respected.

Lil Mike, you've been nothing but a blessing to me. You've shown me who I was meant to be. A good son, father, and provider. You're repaying your mother for all the struggles and sacrifices she made for you over the years. I'm proud of you, son. Thank you so much for allowing me to be a part of your life.

Patrick, another one of my blessings! Anyone you encounter can tell how special you are. You've touched so many lives by just being yourself. Son, thank you for loving me and being a light in my life. Patrick, I love you and I'm proud to call you my son.

Nate, you know what you mean to me. You have one eye and it made you a beast at cutting hair. You're probably the best barber in Indiana, but God doesn't care about that. Son, you have a gift that God wants you to use to bring Him glory and then He'll open some doors for you and allow you to prosper. Think about that, please. We have to quit trying everything else and try God first.

Keaira and Maria, thank you both for allowing God to use you. I don't know who I would be today without you guys ministering to me. Prepare for your awards in heaven. The angels are rejoicing because of your work.

Willie, you're paralyzed. Not because of anything you've done but because of what God wants with you. He'll do anything to slow us down so we can focus on Him. Willie, He didn't slow you down to hinder you. He slowed you down because He wanted to carry you. You have some things in your heart you need to let go of so God can give you peace. A peace that, hopefully, will be passed on to your daughter. I know you're a God-fearing man, but it's time to become a God-seeking man. I love you nephew!

Erica, I used to worry about you so much, but I don't anymore. You've grown into a woman. Please continue to better yourself and keep your brothers together. That's your responsibility now. So, make your Mother and Granny proud.

William, if you don't stop having those kids, I'm going to kick your butt. Seriously, don't have more than you can take care of. If so, you'll just end up hurting them. I just wanted to put that on your mind and let you know that I'm keeping score. I mean tabs on you. LOL.

Ms. Sharday, I know you don't like me, but that's okay. I still want to thank you for being there for Eric. I know you guys don't realize how important of a role you play in our lives, but we know and we appreciate it. I love you, mean girl, and there's nothing you can do about it.

Ms. LaLa and G, thank you both for accepting my son into your family and sharing your mother and father with him. You guys were the family he needed. I pray he's been as much of a blessing to you guys as you've been to him.

AJ, you have a degree that won't use itself. I pray you took that course because you have a passion for it. If so, then turn that passion into action. Start with YouTube. It's all up to you. Remember, the only dreams that can't be fulfilled are those that are never pursued.

Ms. Bre-Bre, I loved your red hair. I'm going to pray success over you in the hair and make-up business. I love your boldness and the desire you have. Put God first and allow Him to take you where He needs you to be.

Shanta and Irene, I could never repay you guys. You gave me the best gifts a man could ever receive. I know I didn't deserve anything from you but you guys raised my sons to love and respect me anyway. Thank you both so much.

If I missed anyone, I'm sorry. Blame it on my old age. I want to say this before I go. For so many years, I thought God was being unfair for having me in here, but we all know if I wasn't in here, I would probably be dead, probably along with some of you. I thank God for allowing me the opportunity to see the men and women that you guys are today. I thank God for the love and support you've showed me and Eric over the years.

We've made it through this because of you. We're alive today because of your prayers. We're alive today because of what Momma instilled in us all: LOVE!!! There's nothing more powerful in the world. Love conquers all. So, continue to allow Momma to smile and laugh that crazy laugh of hers, as she enjoys watching the fruit of her labor. I LOVE YOU GUYS!!!

Let me say this before I go. There's nothing wrong with me. I just love my family and wanted to let you guys know. So, GIRLS don't panic and start trying to figure me out!!!! Just accept the fact that I love and miss you guys.

Peace and God Bless!

Michael Mason

For bulk orders,

please contact Kearia Patterson via phone 219-276-7416

or via email: keariashontell1@yahoo.com.

www.ingramcontent.com/pod-product-compliance
Lightning Source LLC
Chambersburg PA
CBHW071411290426
44108CB00014B/1773